WEALTH BUILDING

Using the Rule of Thirds

Invest Your Money

1/3 in Stocks & Bonds
1/3 in Real Estate & Commodities
1/3 in Liquid Ass~~~

Published by MONEY-POI
2022 Jacob Nayman
All rights reserved.

The knowledge and practices in this book are rooted in Nayman's extensive experience - distilling more than 25 years of expertise in his role as a leading investment adviser to the wealthiest.

D1608143

The Holy Grail of this book
is to achieve two major goals!

Your first major goal:

Increasing your wealth by exploiting
opportunities in the U.S. stock market.

Your second major goal:

Protecting your wealth from possible dangers,
which can pop up at any given time.

To meet these two goals:

You will be introduced
to the best and most effective investment strategies
that suit the U.S. stock market.

As a result of the rapid economic and technological changes around the globe, the middle class has become smaller and smaller each year. The end result of this phenomenon is that in the future the world will be divided into two groups of people:

The rich and established - and everyone else.

As the years go by, if you aren't part of the first group, you will be part of the second one - by default.

Fortunately, there's no predestination.
You can become a member of the rich and established by building your wealth.

This book will provide you with all the necessary knowledge and practical tools you need to exploit the U.S. stock market to generate long-term income.

The investment strategies outlined in this book are based on Nayman's extensive knowledge and experience gained over 25 years in his role as a leading investment and economic adviser to the wealthiest.

The approach described in this book represents a mindset that can be summarized as

HOPE FOR THE BEST

AND

PREPARE FOR THE WORST.

Table of contents

Introduction

Having a good income is not always enough to secure your economic future: for that, you also have to acquire an investment portfolio that will generate long-term income from multiple sources.

There are all sorts of ways to live and retire financially secure. One of the more practical methods is to use your financial savings as a foundation on which to build and preserve your wealth. The profits produced by your investment portfolio will give you the ability to maintain a high standard of living that suits your present and future needs and desires.

For you, as an investor, the stock market and economic reality present fantastic opportunities - and at the same time, significant risks. The Holy Grail of this book is to achieve two important major goals:

Your first major goal – Increasing your wealth by exploiting opportunities in the U.S. stock market.

Your second major goal – Protecting your wealth from possible dangers, which can pop up at any given time.

In order for you to be able to meet these two major goals, you will be introduced to the best stock investment strategies that suit the modern financial markets.

The investment strategies presented in this book will enable you to take advantage of the opportunities created by the stock market, while protecting your money from possible unforeseeable risks.

As a senior financial adviser in the banking system, and an investment portfolio manager in the private sector, I have met thousands of people from many different walks of life.

While these people were very talented in their specific fields, they generally had no understanding at all of the field of financial investments, especially the stock market.

When speaking with layman investors about their financial investments and investing money in the stock market, I used simple, clear language, without glossing over the deeper implications the investment information conveyed. This book has been written following this principle, and is designed for investors who lack an in-depth understanding of the field.

The approach described in this book represents a mindset that can be summarized as:

HOPE FOR THE BEST
AND
PREPARE FOR THE WORST.

Yours,

Jacob Nayman

Chapter 1

Wealth Building

Generating long-term income from multiple sources

The process of building wealth concentrates on how to invest your money in a way that will create an income-generating asset.

Wealth is not defined as your income level. If your yearly income is high, but you spend it all, then you're just keeping up a high standard of living - for now. Wealth is defined by what you save, not what you spend.

How much money do we need?

In order to feel financially secure, most people reply that they need $200,000 a year at least. If you take a couple in their 30s who have two children, it certainly makes sense.

Assuming that the average life expectancy is 80

years, a simple calculation shows that this couple will need an aggregate amount of **$10,000,000** in order to maintain a reasonable standard of living over the next **50** years.

One practical way to generate additional income is to manage our finances in an optimal manner. We can do this by building a private investment portfolio.

IN MY EXPERIENCE

There are two main types of private investors: Equity Investors, who generate additional

income by managing their private investment portfolio. Real estate investors who generate additional revenues by buying homes and offices and leasing them for rent.

**"Never depend on a single income.
Make an investment to create
a second source."**

- Warren Buffett

The process of building wealth is simple:

Make money

Save money

Invest money

The central issue in building and preserving wealth is how to invest the money in a way that will create an income-generating asset.

Conclusions concerning your wealth building

Having a good income is not always enough to secure your economic future: for that, you also have to acquire an investment portfolio that will generate long-term income.

Chapter 2

Investor Mindset

Practice safety

In the process of building and preserving your wealth, it is important from the start that you as an investor, adopt two important principles to guide your mindset:

The first principle is not to make hasty decisions

The basic principle in investments is that you don't *have* to do anything. Even if you do decide to do something, it should be done only with careful planning. The basic cliché is that speed is from the devil - and this is true in the context of investments as well.

In the field of investments, an investor who displays patience and restraint will achieve better results than an investor who is not endowed with the same qualities.

"Success in investing doesn't correlate with IQ... what you need is the temperament to control the urges that get other people into trouble in investing."

- Warren Buffett

The second principle is practicing safety

The central issue in building and preserving wealth is how to invest the money. The safest way to invest your money is to apply the famous golden rule "don't put all your eggs in one basket." If you have built your investment portfolio properly, using the golden rule of diversification, then even a stock market crash shouldn't worry you too much.

A wise investor will do the following:

Invest one-third in stocks and bonds. Invest one-third in real estate, commodities and sectors.

Invest one-third in money and its equivalents.

The rule applied is the rule of thirds

The weight of each investment is one-third.

BE AWARE!

All financial markets are fluid (inflation, currency fluctuations, interest rate changes, etc.): investors who remain passive and don't diversify their investments will likely incur significant losses.

If, for example, you as an investor will invest all your money in a bank deposit with a fixed interest rate, your savings will likely be impacted if the CPI (consumer price index) suddenly rises - the damage will be expressed in reduced purchasing power of your money.

Conclusions concerning your wealth building

Don't make hasty investment decisions.

Practice safety by diversifying your portfolio.

Use the rule of thirds.

Chapter 3

The Trading Platform

Banks vs. stockbrokers

In order to effectively implement asset management, you need to find a good online platform that will allow you to do so.

What are the criteria for a good platform?

Low commissions for performing financial transactions, e.g., buying and selling stock market securities or financial products.

An online connection to your bank account or brokerage account, to be able to sell and buy financial products independently.

Excellent trading platforms that provide added value to the management of your investment portfolio.

Quality of service, measured by availability, professionalism, and the reliability of the information you receive.

There are two financial entities that allow access to buying and selling on the stock exchange.
1) Banks - The commissions are usually high.
2) Stockbrokers - The recommended way to manage stock market-related investments.

While brokerage accounts are managed through a website, every major broker also has a phone number that includes the following services:
1. Service representatives - To answer your questions: for example, regarding the status of a sale you have made - when it will be available for reinvestment.
2. Trading halls - Rooms with many screens that allow representatives to see, in real time, what is happening in the stocks and bonds markets on various stock exchanges around the world.

IN MY EXPERIENCE

If you decide to use a broker, it is better to work with the largest, most stable and best-known broker - the larger the broker, the more assets are backed up.

The advantages of having a financial adviser Support for financial decisions

The adviser has access to the reports prepared by the Economic Department of the financial institution by which they are employed. These reports can provide essential information.

Discounts when buying financial products

An adviser at a large bank or investment company has the power and ability to buy financial products at a discount. Such a discount can sometimes save you a significant amount of money.

Help with buying and selling

If you are a new investor and don't have a lot of experience in buying and selling securities, the adviser can provide you with technical support.

Consultations regarding market trends

You can ask the adviser about market trends and discuss the various issues that arise while you are managing your own portfolio.

BE AWARE!

If you are working with a financial institution that allows you to consult with a licensed investment adviser, you should consider signing an agreement to do so.

IN MY EXPERIENCE

The preferred adviser should be one with many years of experience, and one with whom you communicate well.

Conclusions concerning your wealth building

Low commissions for buying and selling securities and financial products are very important for your financial activity.

If the commissions at the bank are too high, consider working with a big brokerage firm instead.

The advantages of consulting with an adviser lie mainly in their access to central, sophisticated sources of important information.

Chapter 4

Stocks & Bonds

The building blocks of wealth creation

Stocks and bonds are the two main methods of investment in the stock market. Stocks, or shares, are a direct investment: you give money to the company and become a co-owner, with holdings proportional to the percentage of shares you purchased. As a shareholder in the company, you are also entitled to dividends paid by the company.

When you invest in bonds, you are essentially giving a loan to a publicly traded company (corporate bonds) or to the government (government bonds). In return, you receive a guaranteed, predictable cash income which will be paid on a specified future date. The "guaranteed return" is paid by the body that issued the bond (the company or the government).

For example: If you purchased a corporate bond that has five years to maturity and an annual coupon of seven percent, then you are guaranteed to receive a coupon of seven percent in each of those five years. Essentially, you gave the company a loan that gives you a seven percent annual interest rate, and your original bond sum will be returned to you upon completion of the five-year period.

The fundamental difference between stocks and bonds.

Unlike bonds, company shares have no "guaranteed return." In other words, they do not guarantee a predictable cash flow to be paid on a specified future date. When you hold shares, you rely on their market value. When you hold bonds, you have a chance to get the "guaranteed return" even if the company suffers financial difficulties.

There are three criteria to consider prior to the acquisition of bonds:

1. The yield to maturity - The annual return to the investor, if the bond is held until maturity.

2. The average life of the bond - The average duration, in years, of the bond. The longer the term, the riskier the bond.

3. The bond rating - A rating that indicates the probability that the borrower (the corporation) will meet its obligations and return the promised interest as well as the money invested.

BE AWARE!

Solid bonds have to meet two criteria:

First, there should be no more than five years to maturity; and second, their rating should be A or higher.

Government vs. corporate bonds:

Corporate bonds are rated according to their level of risk. The rating is given by professional companies who specialize in the topic. The rating provides investors with information regarding the risk of investing in various bonds.

If the bond rating is low (for example BBB), it means that the probability that you could lose all your money is high. The expected interest on such low-rated bonds is very high - some investors are willing to take the chance and buy low-rated (dangerous) bonds: the compensation for the additional risk that those investors take is called the "risk premium." This is why corporate junk bonds are also called high-yield bonds.

IN MY EXPERIENCE

Compared to corporate bonds, government bonds

are always safer. The government can always print more money to meet its obligations, while companies depend on their financial strength to meet their obligations.

Conclusions concerning your wealth building

A stock (also known as equity) is a security that represents the ownership of a fraction of a corporation.

A bond is a fixed-income instrument that represents a loan made by an investor to a borrower.

Unlike bonds, company shares have no "guaranteed return."

Chapter 5

Play It Safe — Diversify
Get higher rewards with minimal risk

The only situation in which you should be willing to tolerate higher risk is one in which you expect to be rewarded with higher profits.

Wealth management should follow the same logic: if a higher risk doesn't carry the potential of a higher return, then naturally you should invest in something less risky.

In wealth management you have two powerful and effective tools to reduce your portfolio risks: asset allocation, and buying indexes instead of individual stocks.

1. Asset allocation

Asset allocation is an investment strategy that aims to balance risk and reward by apportioning a portfolio's assets in different investment channels (stocks, commodities, bonds, and cash).

How does asset allocation reduce risk?

Asset allocation helps investors reduce risk through diversification. The returns of stocks, bonds, commodities and cash do not move in unison. Market conditions can lead to one asset class outperforming during a given timeframe, but cause another to underperform. This kind of market behavior balances and reduces the volatility of the entire investment portfolio.

For example: You can invest your money by applying the rule of thirds to asset allocation:

Invest one-third in real estate and commodities

Invest one-third in stocks and bonds

Invest one-third in money and its equivalents

2. Buy indexes instead of individual stocks

The better alternative to buying individual stocks is to buy an index that represents the investment channel in which we want to allocate our money. For example, instead of picking and buying three or four stocks that belong to the technology sector, we can buy an ETF (exchange-traded fund) that represents the Nasdaq 100 index. This allows you to buy a small piece of the stock of 100 different companies in the Nasdaq sector at once, with one single investment. This also will eliminate the specific risks of the stocks in your portfolio.

The total risk of a security is the sum of two types of risks:

1. **Market risk**

    Market risk is the product of macroeconomic factors, such as a sharp rise in interest rates, inflation, deflation, a shrinking GDP, a large rise in unemployment, a major geopolitical crisis, and more.

2. **Specific security risk**

    Specific security risks derive from specific negative events such as strikes, mismanagement, embezzlement, or risks that decrease the company's profit due to unexpected events. This type of risk can lead to a sharp drop in the price of the company's shares.

How can specific risk be eliminated?

Research shows that a portfolio that contains over 20 different securities disables the specific risk element, making it irrelevant. The results of the research performed also lead to another amazing and very important conclusion: if you invest in a small number of securities, for example five, and not a large number of securities - at least 20, you expose yourself to high risk **without** the reward of higher returns.

BE AWARE!

When you invest your money by buying indexes or sectors you eliminate the specific risk.

By their very nature, indexes are less risky because they spread their investment across many securities. However, it is important to note that even if you entirely eliminate the specific risk in your investment portfolio, you are still exposed to the market risk.

Conclusions concerning your wealth building

There are two powerful tools to reduce your portfolio risks: The first tool is asset allocation. The second tool is buying indexes instead of individual stocks.

Greater risks should be taken only if the potential return is high. If not, the risk should be avoided.

If you invest in individual stocks, you expose yourself to high risk **without** the reward of higher returns.

Chapter 6

Buy Index ETFs

Don't pick specific stocks

It is highly recommended that you invest your money using ETFs, and not by investing in specific stocks. Investments in specific stocks/companies have no place in the construction and management of assets. Beginning investors as well as more experienced investors are advised not to try to invest in any particular company.

What is an index ETF?

An exchange-traded fund (ETF) is a basket of securities that trades on an exchange just like a stock does. Typically, ETFs will track a particular index, sector, commodity, or other asset. With an index ETF, you, as an investor, gain exposure to numerous securities in a single transaction.

The first ETF was the SPDR S&P 500 ETF (SPY), which tracks the S&P 500 Index.

The stock's / ETF's ticker symbol

Each stock traded on the U.S. stock exchange is associated with a ticker symbol. The ticker consists of a number of letters that are usually reminiscent of the name of the company that issued the shares. The ticker is used by investors in any case in which it is necessary to specify the specific stock, for example when issuing a buy or sell order or when searching for information about the share price. For example: the ticker for the SPDR S&P 500 ETF is SPY.

IN MY EXPERIENCE

An important consideration when buying ETFs is their marketability - the ease with which you can buy and sell them at market price when you choose.

How to choose the best ETFs?

When you decide to buy an ETF in a specific sector, a specific commodity or a specific index, you will find that there is more than one financial entity that manages such an ETF, so your question will be which ETF to choose from a list of ETFs.

The golden rule that should guide you is to choose the ETF from the two biggest ETFs in the investment product sought.

For example, let's say you decided to purchase an ETF on gold, and there are at least 10 ETFs from different financial entities that can be purchased. The rule of thumb to use is to examine the two largest entities, in terms of asset management scope, and to invest in the one with the lower management fees.

Why is investing through ETFs better than buying individual stocks?
Reduced portfolio risk

When you buy ETFs on indexes, the volatility (risk) of the investment portfolio is much lower than when you invest in specific companies.

Reduced portfolio fees

ETFs offer low expense ratios and fewer broker commissions compared to buying the stocks individually. The low fees mean that more of your investment stays with you, rather than being drained off by the investment house.

Improved focus

What should lead your investment decisions in the stock market is not the question of which individual stocks to pick and buy, but what investment indexes/sectors are the best ones to invest in.

Time savings

In order to invest in individual stocks and do it well, you must invest a great deal of time doing research and a great deal of attention to monitor the stocks.

Conclusions concerning your wealth building

Buying ETFs on indexes enable you easily to implement the golden rule - "don't put all your eggs in one basket."

Buying ETFs on sectors or indexes diversifies your investments and considerably reduces the volatility of your portfolio.

Buying ETFs on indexes or sectors reduces your fees.

Chapter 7

Stocks and the Economy

Cyclical and non-cyclical sectors

In wealth building, the distinction between cyclical and non-cyclical sectors is important in the process of allocating assets.

For example, suppose that stock market investors think the economy will recover quickly because the price of petroleum is going to decrease considerably. In that case, stocks in cyclical sectors such as banks or cars will benefit from a positive sentiment.

Cyclical vs. non-cyclical stocks

The terms cyclical and non-cyclical refer to how closely a company's share price is tied to the changes and fluctuations in the economy. Cyclical companies are affected by broad economic changes that do not affect non-cyclical companies.

Cyclical stocks

Cyclical stocks and their companies are affected by the economy. When the economy shows positive signs, the price of cyclical stocks will go up. But an economic downturn will have a negative effect on their stock prices.

Cyclical stock companies sell goods and services that the general public buys when the economy is doing well, but reduces or stops purchasing when there is an economic downturn.

For example, airlines, restaurants, hotel chains, and cars are goods and services that people consume less during slowed economic growth. As a result of this drop in spending, the revenues of companies that produce and sell these goods and services fall. This puts negative pressure on their stock prices.

Non-cyclical stocks

Non-cyclical stocks are profitable regardless of economic trends because they produce or distribute **basic** goods and services that consumers always require. Examples of basic goods are things such as food, electric power, water, and gas.

Utility company stocks are a great example. People always need power and heat, so even when economic growth slows, non-cyclical stocks can outperform cyclical stocks.

The distinction between cyclical and non-cyclical sectors is important in the process of allocating assets.

Secular and cyclical trends

A secular trend is a long-term trend that indicates that a particular sector of the economy is changing. A prominent example of a secular change was the disappearance of the horse and buggy with the advent of the automobile industry. A cyclical trend occurs rapidly. Therefore, the terms secular and cyclical trends can refer to long-term or short-term trends in the economy and in the stock market, respectively.

A secular change is a company's long-term direction of development in a specific industry, whereas a cyclical trend is the short-term direction of the stock prices in a specific industry. We can predict that, in the long run, the technology industry will be in a secular upswing. In contrast, the stocks for this industry in the short-term have cyclical ups and downs.

IN MY EXPERIENCE

We can also profit from cyclical short-term trends where the prices of shares are volatile.

Conclusions concerning your wealth building

Cyclical or non-cyclical stocks refers to the correlation between stocks and the economy.

A cyclical trend is the short-term direction of the stock prices in a specific industry.

If we want to take advantage of market volatility, we should concentrate on short-term cyclical sector trends.

Chapter 8

Define Your Preferences

Amount of money, time frame, and level of risk

Before you implement an asset allocation strategy, you have to define what your preferences are as an investor. Your investment portfolio should be built in accordance with your desires and needs; to accomplish this, you need to address the following issues:

The amount of money

You have to determine the appropriate amount of money to invest in the capital markets. To do this, you must also consider your other assets and the level of risk to which they are exposed.

The investment horizon

The longer the investment horizon, the higher the level of risk you can afford to be exposed to, since your investments will have plenty of time to ride out the market's short-term volatility. Accordingly, the potential to gain higher returns will be greater.

If, for example, you know in advance that you are going to purchase a house within the next two years – then you shouldn't use this money to invest in the capital market. Why? Because it is possible that the capital market will decline sharply during those two years: since you will be forced to sell your investment in order to buy the house, you will not be able to wait for the market to rise and correct itself, and you will lose money on your investment.

Exposure to risk and required return

As an investor, you should decide what weight (percentage) to give the risky and the solid parts of your portfolio. A simple investment strategy is to keep all of your money in U.S. treasury bonds, which have a guaranteed return: the obvious advantage of this strategy is that it's a safe investment with almost no risk, while the disadvantage is that the return on such an investment will accordingly be very low.

If, however, you are an investor who is willing to take some risk, investment in stocks, commodities and corporate bonds will increase your chances of earning more money.

IN MY EXPERIENCE

The relationship between reward and risk is a double-edged sword: to profit more, you have to be willing to take more risk.

Suppose you have $200,000, and meet with an investment company that wants to manage your money. If they ask you, "How much do you want to earn?" your immediate, instinctive answer would probably be, "As much as I can!" But what are the implications of such an answer?

If, for example, you want to gain an average yearly return of 30 percent, then it's possible that you could actually lose 30 percent. Why? Because your investment portfolio will need to consist of securities with higher risk; for example, a greater number of shares relative to government bonds. If you want to gain only 10 percent, the possible loss will be adjusted accordingly: your investment portfolio will consist of many government bonds, with a smaller exposure to stocks.

Exposure to foreign markets and currencies

You also need to decide whether you want to expose your investment portfolio to domestic and/or foreign, developed, or emerging markets. Note that if you buy ETFs traded in a foreign country, in most cases they will be influenced by the currency exchange of that country; therefore, your investment returns will also be influenced by the exchange rate. In other words, buying ETFs on overseas stock indexes exposes you to foreign currency volatility.

Distribution by geographical location

Developed countries: The U.S, several countries in Europe, Australia, Japan.

Developing countries: China, Several countries in Asia, Brazil, Russia.

Investing in developing countries is more risky (more volatile) than investing in developed countries, and their weight in the portfolio should therefore be smaller.

For example,
    One-third in the U.S.
One-third in Europe.
One-third in emerging markets.
The same is true for bonds.

Conclusions concerning your wealth building

The relationship between return and risk is a double-edged sword: to profit more, you have to be willing to take more risk.

The longer the investment horizon, the higher the level of risk you can afford to be exposed to.

When you buy ETFs traded in a foreign country, they will be also influenced by the currency volatility.

Chapter 9

The Rule of Thirds

Asset allocation

Asset allocation strategy attempts to balance risk and reward by adjusting the percentage of each asset in the investment portfolio according to your personal preferences.

The main assumption in asset allocation is that the investment in different assets results in diversification, which reduces the overall risk in your investment portfolio while maintaining the level of the expected return.

THE RULE OF THIRDS

A wise investor will do the following:
Invest one-third in stocks and bonds.

Invest one-third in real estate, commodities and volatile sectors.

Invest one-third in money and its equivalents.

Each of the three components of the portfolio has a different role.

The "liquid" third of the portfolio

The liquid component has two objectives:

The first objective is to reduce the risk exposure of the overall portfolio. The second objective is to have the ability to exploit opportunities when stock market prices plunge considerably.

Holding cash and money equivalents is preferred for two reasons:

First, by maintaining high liquidity, you create a reality in which your portfolio exposure to the volatility/risk of the financial markets is reduced.

Second, when the markets fall considerably – liquidity gives you the ability to exploit opportunities and buy securities at an attractive price, using ETFs.

Financial products considered cash and cash equivalents:

- Deposit accounts
- Short-term government bonds
- Money market funds
- Certificates of deposit (CDs - including foreign currency)

IN MY EXPERIENCE

When there is a major crisis in the financial markets and the prices of stocks and bonds reach bottom / unprecedented lows, opportunities are created.

When there is a major crisis in the financial markets you can take advantage and pick stocks and bonds at good prices. You will be in a better position to do this if you have high liquidity - money that has been sitting and waiting outside the financial markets.

The "market" third of the portfolio

The expectation is that the "market" component of your portfolio will produce returns/profits close to the market benchmark.

The "market" component of the portfolio incorporates investments that don't require dynamic handling.

Financial products that can be included in the "market" component of the portfolio:

- ETFs on sectors such as banks and technology.
- ETFs on major indexes such as the S&P 500 index, Dow Jones, DAX 100.
- Government bonds: medium-term, with an average maturity of up to five years.
- Corporate bonds: with high ratings (A or higher); medium-term, with an average maturity of up to five years.

The "alpha" third of the portfolio

In the "alpha" component, you adjust your portfolio to include the indexes, assets, or sectors that are riskier and show the most potential for gains. The expectation is that the "alpha" component of your portfolio will outperform the market benchmark. The "alpha" component of the portfolio is composed of investments that demand a more dynamic approach.

Financial products that can be included in the alpha component of the portfolio

- Stocks
- Crypto — digital currency
- Corporate junk bonds with high yields
- ETFs on REITs (commercial or residential real estate)
- Convertible bonds, warrants, options
- ETFs on commodities such as gold, petroleum and agriculture products
- ETFs on small cap stocks — such as the Russell 2000 Index

Conclusions concerning your wealth building

A wise investor will do the following:

Invest one-third in stocks and bonds.

Invest one-third in real estate, commodities and volatile sectors.

Invest one-third in money and its equivalents.

Chapter 10

Portfolio Construction
Implementing the rule of thirds

There are two advantages to building your portfolio using the rule of thirds. First, the technical management of the portfolio is simplified and therefore easier to control. Second, it's easier to measure the performance of the portfolio against market benchmarks.

Portfolio Construction

Stage 1: Determining the characteristics of the portfolio

Parameters: the sum of money to invest, the level of risk, the investment horizon, and the investment strategy.

For example:

The sum of money: $600,000.
The level of risk: up to 50 percent.
The investment horizon: 20 years.
The investment strategy: The rule of thirds.

Stage 2: The liquid third of the portfolio

Sum of cash and cash equivalents – $200,000
The goal – To reduce portfolio risk exposure while exploiting opportunities in the financial markets.

The money should be invested in liquid products such as: cash, short-term bonds, deposits.

Warning!

The securities mentioned here are only examples and do not represent suggestions or any recommendation for what you should or should not invest in. It is highly recommended that you build your private investment portfolio with the help of a licensed financial adviser.

Stage 3: Building the "market" third of your portfolio

Sum of ETFs - $200,000

The goal - The expected returns should be close to the returns of the "market portfolio."

ETFs that are considered to closely represent the "market portfolio benchmark" are the S&P 500 or Dow index in the U.S., the DAX index in Germany, the FTSE 100 in England, Nikkei 225 in Japan, and the CAC 40 index in France.

For example:

The risky component (50 percent) - $100,000

$33,333 in an ETF on the S&P 500.

$33,333 in an ETF on the big banks sector in the U.S.

$33,333 in an ETF on the NASDAQ.

The solid component (50 percent) - $100,000

$33,333 in an ETF on government linked bonds.

$33,333 in an ETF on medium-term corporate linked bonds (rated at least A+).

$33,333 in an ETF on medium-term municipal bonds (rated at least A+).

How inflationary expectations can impact your investments

If there is a reason to expect inflationary pressures, this may affect your decisions regarding asset allocation. You can invest more money in IL (inflation-linked) corporate and government bonds in your investment portfolio.

Building the solid market component of your portfolio

All of the bonds in the solid component should meet two criteria: first, the bonds should have an average maturity of five years or less; and second, the corporate bonds should have high ratings (A or higher).

Stage 4: Building the alpha third

Sum of ETFs - $200,000

The goal: The expected return on the alpha component should have the potential to **outperform** the returns of the "market portfolio." The alpha component will be built from more volatile/risky assets.

For example:

$66,666 in a REIT real estate ETF.

$66,666 in commodity ETFs such as: gold, petroleum, agricultural products.

$66,666 in short term investments in volatile sectors.

Other options:

- Crypto - digital currency
- ETFs on small cap stocks - such as the Russell 2000 Index
- ETFs on the semiconductor industry sector
- ETFs on the defense industry sector
- ETFs on the clean energy sector

Insights regarding the portfolio

Minimized costs and minimized risk in the "market" component

The first advantage is that the "market" component is composed of passively managed ETFs, so the managing fees charged, as well as the transaction costs, are considerably less expensive than those incurred buying individual stocks. The second advantage is that the "market" component is composed of ETFs that approximately represent the "market portfolio"; therefore, there is close to optimal diversification of the portfolio, ensuring reduced portfolio volatility.

Maximize returns in the "alpha" component

The alpha component consists of investments that are riskier than the "market" investments. The only justification for the higher risk is the assumption that the expected overall returns will beat the "market" benchmark.

Minimize volatility in the "alpha" component

Commodities such as gold, crude oil and agricultural products can be held in the investment portfolio and used as an insurance policy against inflation or periods of high market volatility. Investing in commodities can be considered an effective strategy to reduce volatility.

Exposure to foreign markets and currencies

If you buy ETFs traded in a foreign country, they, in most cases, will be influenced by the currency exchange of that country. Therefore, buying ETFs on overseas stock indexes exposes you to foreign currency volatility.

BE AWARE!

You can also choose to invest in sectors that match your personal values and desires.

Expressing personal values in the "alpha" component

If, for example, saving the planet is important to you, you can express this value by investing some of your money in an ETF that deals with less harmful, renewable energy. If you love the military, you can invest in an ETF related to the army. If you are an advanced technology and robotics freak, you can act accordingly.

Conclusions concerning your wealth building

Implementing the rule of thirds in your portfolio will enable you to minimize costs and volatility and outperform the market benchmark.

Chapter 11

When is the Right Time to Buy?

"The best chance to deploy capital is when things are going down."

Warren Buffett

As an investor who manages your own personal investment portfolio, you should decide during which periods of time to buy and sell ETFs.

You can think of ETFs like a train running along the market's trend line (i.e., the "tracks"). You, the investor in these ETFs, are not the train driver, but a passenger who can choose when to get on the train and when to get off; in addition to buying and selling, you can also decide how much money to invest. The return of the ETFs is not necessarily equal to your return: your return will depend only on your financial decisions, which determine the timing and the amount of your investment.

BE AWARE!

There is a distinction between buying long-term ETFs as long-term investment — for at least 10 years — and buying ETFs for the short term (less than one year).

In the "alpha" component of your portfolio, you can choose to invest some of your money to profit from volatile sectors.

When you want to invest your money for the long run, you can adopt Warren Buffet's strategy:

"I will tell you how to become rich.
Close the doors.

**Be fearful when others are greedy.
Be greedy when others are fearful."**

Which sectors should we focus on for the long run - in order to achieve alpha returns? The answer is straightforward: the sector or sectors whose prices have decreased considerably (over 35 percent).

If, for example, the technological sector in the market has gone down by 32 percent and the inflation is at eight percent, we can consider buying an ETF on the Nasdaq - after it goes down 40 (32 + 8) percent. If it continues to go down - for example an additional 10 percent, we can buy more. There is a high probability that after several years, the technological sector will rise again and we will enjoy nice profits from our original investment.

When you see that the market is coming close to its peak, i.e., the market is saturated, you can decide to materialize some of your long-term investments by moving some of the money to less risky investments, namely solid ETFs.

When your investment strategy is based on short-term profits (less than one year), you can use the cyclical short-term volatility in the stock market to your advantage. The right conditions for using this kind of investment strategy are described in Chapter 14.

If, for example, we buy an ETF of shares in the banking sector after their prices drop considerably, (five percent or more), we can predict that there is a good chance (if the right conditions exist) that the sector will enjoy a positive sentiment in the foreseeable future and its prices will go up. We don't know why or when it will happen - it can take weeks or months before the positive sentiment is expected to return to this sector.

The underlying logic is that in the foreseeable future, the weeks or few months after you buy the sector stocks, something positive will impact the market, and this sector will rise again. When it does, then it will be the right time for us to materialize our short-term profits.

Conclusions concerning your wealth building

If you have the opportunity to buy securities in a sector or an index at low prices, then increase your exposure to this index or sector.

Implement Warren Buffet's golden rule:

"Be fearful when others are greedy.
 Be greedy when others are fearful."

Chapter 12

Rebalancing
Preserving the Rule of Thirds

In the process of wealth building, one of the most important actions is to maintain the portfolio asset allocation.

IN MY EXPERIENCE

When you have a managed portfolio, the investment company does the rebalancing for you.

Why is maintaining the rule of thirds important?

It enables you to implement the golden rule - "Don't put all your eggs in one basket"

The rule of thirds:

One-third in stocks and bonds.

One-third in real estate, commodities and volatile sectors.

One-third in money and its equivalents.

Balancing your portfolio means buying and selling securities in a way that will return the portfolio to its desired risk levels.

For example, due to an increase in share prices in the stock market, the "market" component and the "alpha" component in the portfolio can grow considerably. Let's assume that after three months they grow from 33 percent to 40 percent each. So now we have a portfolio with only 20 percent liquidity, not the 33 percent you intended to have when you were first building your investment portfolio. What should you do in this scenario to rebalance your portfolio?

In the process of rebalancing, we will sell seven percent of the alpha component and seven percent of the market component, and the money from the sales will be reinvested in relevant products in the liquid component. The end result of this rebalancing process will be a balanced portfolio that maintains the rule of thirds.

The maintenance process:

Check your investment portfolio every three months to see if it meets the rule of thirds. If necessary, rebalance to maintain the desired asset allocation.

When the ETFs go down – buy more shares to rebalance.

When the ETFs go up – sell some of the stocks and materialize profits to rebalance.

Conclusions concerning your wealth building

Rebalancing involves periodically buying or selling assets in a portfolio to maintain its original or desired level of asset allocation.

In the process of rebalancing every three months, maintain the rule of thirds.

Chapter 13

Risk Management
An instrument that protects your money

In the context of maintaining your standard of living, you can look at yourself as a "machine" that makes money. You usually wake up in the morning, brush your teeth, eat breakfast, and go to work. While at work you generate income that enables you to maintain the standard of living to which you are accustomed.

If the machine malfunctions - i.e., you get sick - two things happen: the "machine," in most cases, ceases to produce income; and your expenses increase, due to the costs of your medical treatment.

There are seven situations in which the" machine" will stop working: two are related to positive situations, and five are not. The positive situations include age-appropriate retirement from work or voluntary departure from the workplace. The five negative situations include permanent loss of the ability to work; disease; disability; the need for long-term nursing care; and death. To protect yourself in case of one of these five negative situations, you must prepare a sufficient defense ahead of time, so that your standard of living, and that of your loved ones, won't be affected.

For example, if you suffer a severe injury and are unable to work, lack of appropriate insurance coverage may leave your family financially unprotected. As a result, your standard of living can be severely impacted. Since the level of government aid is minimal, in some circumstances you may even find yourself at the poverty level.

IN MY EXPERIENCE
Our defense system — also known as insurance - is our lifeline in situations in which our health is affected.

Why does insurance coverage actually protect your wealth?

For example, if you need very expensive surgery, one that can only be performed abroad, or one that costs hundreds of thousands of dollars - a good health insurance plan will cover all of the expenses involved. Insurance, therefore, enables you to protect your health, and even your life. In the situation above, what would you do without it?

The answer is simple: you would probably go broke. In an emergency situation, if you don't have an insurance policy to protect you and your loved ones, you'll likely be forced to use all of the money at your disposal, even taking out loans and spending your last savings, to fund the medical care necessary for survival.

However, when you have insurance protection, money **doesn't come out** of your pockets - instead, all of the costs are covered by the insurance company.

The bottom line is this: the purpose of insurance coverage is to protect yourself from financial crises, and in some situations, even financial collapse.

Conclusions concerning your wealth building

The general premise of insurance is that you, as a customer buy peace of mind — while the insurance company buys your risk.

The protection afforded by insurance coverage can be considered a risk management tool that protects your wealth.

Chapter 14

The Short-Term Profit Strategy

Exploiting cyclical trends

Years ago, when I was working as an investment adviser in the banking system, a senior investment adviser with over 30 years of professional experience approached me and asked me to do her a favor.

She gave me the details of her bank account, and asked me to buy stocks for her by purchasing an ETF on the S&P 500 index that represented the 500 leading companies in the stock market.

Her golden rule for investment decisions was that if the stock market went down considerably, she would buy the ETF on the S&P 500 index, and days or weeks later, when the stock market prices went up considerably, she would sell the ETF on the S&P 500 index and materialize her short-term profits.

After having materialized her profits, she waited

patiently for a drop in stock market prices. Once the prices had decreased considerably, she again bought the ETF on the S&P 500 index.

Over time, she also gave me the bank accounts of her mother and daughter and asked me to do the same for them.

I used this golden rule for buying and selling ETFs for the senior investment adviser and her family over five years, and noticed that it produced very profitable results.

THE GOLDEN RULE
(THE SHORT-TERM PROFIT STRATEGY)

Buy an ETF on a sector or an index
when its price drops considerably.
Sell the ETF on the sector or the index
when its price rises considerably.

There are three conditions that should be present in the stock market to justify using the short-term (less than a year) profit strategy.

Condition number 1
The "Safety Net" condition

When you invest money in the stock market, you can be certain that the most powerful economic forces in the world will support the stock market if needed. These powerful economic forces are the American Federal Reserve and the U.S. Treasury.

The investors in the financial markets know that if something bad happens to the economy or the financial markets, policy-makers will intervene. They will use any weapon at their disposal to support the economy and the financial markets.

Condition number 2
The lack of attractive alternatives to the stock market

The major traditional alternatives to investing in stocks are investing in bonds or treasury notes.

When the interest rates that the treasury notes offer and the yields on bonds are low and not attractive, then the stock market (even if riskier) becomes more attractive. In such an environment, the stock market becomes the most attractive investment for investors compared to other financial alternatives.

Condition number 3
Rotation of positive sentiment between sectors

If you track stock market data over the years, an interesting phenomenon becomes apparent - after the value of a specific sector (let's say the technological sector) enjoys positive sentiment and its prices rise to new records, investors have a tendency to look for other sectors that may have been relatively undervalued by investors, whose prices are relatively attractive and more reasonable for purchasing (for example, the bank sector).

This phenomenon, in which the "undervalued sector" becomes the preferred sector, is referred to as the rotation of positive sentiment between sectors.

In normal times, the rotation of positive sentiment

between sectors can take an average of three months. In a more volatile stock market, it can take weeks and even days.

The third assumption gives us, as investors, the ability to produce **alpha returns** on our financial investment. It also supports practicing the short-term profit strategy.

The short-term profit strategy is used also by leading hedge funds and investment banks.

Alpha returns

The alpha of an investment is the excess return of that investment relative to the return of a benchmark index. For example, if the S&P 500 index rises by three precent in one month, you invested your money in the technology sector, and the Nasdaq rose seven percent over the same period of time, your investment in the technology sector created an alpha of four precent.

BE AWARE!

If you decide to act in accordance with the short-term strategy, you must be aware of the three conditions and make sure that they are all upheld.

The short-term profit strategy as part of an investment portfolio

The short-term investment strategy can be used as a standalone strategy, especially if you have only thousands of dollars at your disposal for investment in the stock market. However, it can also be used as the alpha component of your investment portfolio. If it is a part of an investment portfolio, it shouldn't be more than 20 percent of your overall investments.

Conclusions concerning your wealth building

The short-term profit strategy

Buy an ETF on a sector or an index when its price drops considerably.

Sell the ETF when its price rises considerably.

Chapter 15

Focus on Sectors or Indexes

Don't pick specific stocks

The question that should guide your investment decisions in the stock market is not the question of which individual stocks to pick and buy, but what indexes or sectors are the best ones to invest in.

In our days investors know in advance that policymakers (the Federal Reserve and the U.S. Treasury) will use their tremendous power to support the economy and financial markets if their intervention is needed. This policy-maker behavior helps produce positive cyclical trends in the stock market.

IN MY EXPERIENCE

We can exploit positive trends in the equity market to our advantage to gain profits. To do so, we can use the short-term profit strategy.

Why, when buying stocks for the short term, should you focus on sectors or indexes and not on picking specific stocks?

There are three main reasons why short-term investments (for less than one year) should be made in sectors or indexes (using ETFs) and not in specific stocks.

Reason 1

Picking stocks is not an easy job. You may get the sector call right, but the stock call wrong. Policy-maker actions don't support specific stocks: they support the macro behavior of the economy and the financial markets. It should be assumed that the actions taken by policy-makers will positively impact the entire stock market.

If you buy a specific security in the stock market, then even if the stock market displays an overall rise (because the policy-makers for example, injected money), the price of your specific stock could remain the same or even go down.

Therefore, if you want to increase your chances of profiting, the solution is to invest in a general index (like the S&P 500 index) or in sectors (such as banks or the Nasdaq), and not in specific stocks.

Reason 2

When you buy stocks to hold for the long run, you can use a more aggressive strategy than when you invest for the short term (less than one year).

An investor who plans on holding a particular security for several years has time to recover any loss in value, which can often happen with aggressive or risky investments. In contrast, short term investments require less risk. Buying and holding ETFs on an index or a sector gives you this preferred, less risky investment.

Reason 3

Economic indicators (consumer confidence, the GDP, the rate of unemployment, inflation, other economic events) impact different sectors in the stock market in different ways.

Sectors that can be impacted include, for example – technology, banking, consumption, airline companies, etc. Buying and selling ETFs on sectors enables us, as investors, to exploit those macroeconomic events to our benefit and make short term profits. Moreover, it gives us the ability to create alpha returns, which are higher than the general stock market returns.

The question that should guide your decisions is, what indexes or sectors are the best ones to invest in.

Sector-based investments using ETFs can help you, as an investor, to accomplish two important goals:

First - to provide targeted exposure to a sector, while minimizing your exposure to stock-specific risk.

Second - to deliver alpha by overweighting winning sectors and underweighting losers.

For example, rather than selecting three or four companies from the technological sector, you can focus on the entire sector and buy an ETF on the Nasdaq in order to capture a positive trend in the technology sector.

Conclusions concerning your wealth building

If you want to create short term profits, investing your money in indexes and sectors using ETFs is a better strategy than investing in individual stocks.

Deliver alpha by overweighting winning sectors and underweighting losers.

Use ETFs to benefit from the positive interventions made by policy-makers.

Chapter 16

The Value of Unknown Information

The big advantage

As an investor, your strategy can be to "stay on the fence" until the sky in the economy and the financial markets clears. This period can take years - and you, like most investors, probably have a fear of missing out.

The alternative to "staying on the fence" is to practice an investment strategy (for the long run and for the short run) that exploits opportunities in the stock market, and to do so mainly by buying ETFs on sectors or indexes when their prices go down considerably and selling the ETFs when the prices go up considerably.

In this strategy you invest **without** any specific knowledge or information about what will happen in the future or when.

BE AWARE!

When you invest without any specific knowledge you assume that something will happen in the foreseeable or distant future that will impact the stock market in a positive way.

NEW, previously unknown information vs. known information

In the stock market, the value of known information is considered to be near zero.

What moves the markets up or down is always new, unexpected information.

117

Why?

There is always the assumption that the present prices of shares in the stock market already reflect future expectations.

Therefore, what moves the markets up or down is always new, unexpected information. We can clearly see this effect when economic data is released.

If, for example, the unemployment rate rises considerably, higher **than was expected** by the investors in the market, we are likely to see a negative effect on stock prices.

If the rate of unemployment is as expected, then this information in itself will probably not impact the stock market at all - given, of course, that other economic and financial factors behave as expected.

When we buy an ETF in a sector whose stock prices were falling considerably, we assume that sometime in the future something positive will happen in the economy or the firm's profitability (although we don't know when or why), and that this specific sector will experience positive sentiment that will lead to a rally or correction of its stock prices.

The amazing thing is that there is no certainty regarding this information when we buy the stocks, but the value of this unknown information is high; and when the positive impact materializes, we can sell our stocks with a nice profit.

If the opposite was true, and investors knew in advance exactly when and what positive things are expected to happen in a specific sector, this positive information would be reflected in the present, in higher stock prices. Therefore, when the good things actually happen, they won't impact the prices of stocks at all – the prices of the stocks you purchased already embodied this good news.

Conclusions concerning your wealth building

Paradoxically, our ability to profit as investors is increased when we buy stocks without knowing when they will rise again or what exactly will impact them.

When we buy, we assume that something good will happen in the future. We don't know what or when, and neither do the other investors in the market

Chapter 17

What is Moving the Markets?

Policy-makers' big impact

The economy and the financial markets in our days are completely controlled by policy-makers: if the economy or the financial markets are in trouble, then the policy-makers (the Federal Reserve and U.S. Treasury) will use all the weapons at their disposal to change the situation for the better.

Who are the policy-makers?
The U.S. Treasury

The U.S. Treasury directly represents the agenda of the politicians. The Treasury is responsible for the decisions that impact the economy — such as the transfer of trillions of dollars to individuals, households and businesses that lost their income due to the disastrous effects of the Covid-19 pandemic.

The Federal Reserve

The Federal Reserve is the central banking system of the United States of America.

What are the main goals of the policymakers?
In the economy:

In the United States, the Federal Reserve has four main economic goals: to achieve low unemployment (close to five percent); to maintain stable prices (two - three percent inflation per year); to keep interest rates relatively low; and to keep the GDP growing. If needed, it also provides banks with liquidity that enables them to operate in a "healthy" way.

In the financial markets:

Policy-makers contribute to the stability of prices in the bond market and in the stock market to prevent their collapse. Preventing the collapse of these very important financial markets protects also pension funds.

How can interest rates impact your investment decisions?

If you know that the solid channel offers you a high interest rate with a very low risk, then you presumably will invest most of your money in solid investments, such as government bonds. When interest rates are high, your motivation to expose your money to risky investments, such as stocks, will be low.

The opposite is also true: the lower the interest rates are, the more willing you will be to take more risks in order to generate higher returns, and the higher your level of exposure to risky assets will be. In low interest rate conditions, the demand for risky assets is higher, and the prices of equities, accordingly, are also higher.

BE AWARE!
Today's capital market price incorporates future expectations.

The main weapons used by policy-makers and their impact on the financial markets.

Quantitative easing (QE)

QE is a monetary policy strategy used by central banks, such as the Federal Reserve. Under QE, a central bank purchases securities in an attempt to reduce interest rates, increase the supply of money and drive more lending to consumers and businesses. The goal is to expand economic activity. In the context of our investment portfolio, the most important thing that QE policy creates is a positive sentiment in the stock market, which elevates stocks prices.

Quantitative tightening (QT)

Quantitative tightening is a contractionary monetary policy applied by a central bank to decrease the amount of liquidity within the economy. The effect of QT is increased interest rates that help to slow or keep the domestic currency from inflation.

In the context of our investment portfolio, implementation of QT policy has a negative impact on the prices of shares in the stock market.

Conclusions concerning your wealth building

If the economy shows signs of an impending economic slowdown/recession, the Federal Reserve will use the QE policy to lower interest rates and positively impact stocks.

If the economy shows signs of overheating that has the potential to lead to inflation pressures, the Federal Reserve will use the QT policy to raise interest rates and negatively impact stocks.

Chapter 18

Leading Market Indicators:
The impact on interest rates

The indicators presented here all have a common denominator: they must be analyzed over a period of time, so the direction of their trend is revealed.

When you analyze them over time, it is particularly important to check how an increase or decrease in specific indicators impacts inflationary pressures and hence causes an increase or decrease in interest rates.

IN MY EXPERIENCE

If interest rates are rising, the influence on the stock market will be negative. If the interest rates are going down, or stable, there will be a positive impact on your portfolio.

What are the leading financial indicators that impact interest rates?

1. Consumer Price Index

The consumer price index (CPI) measures changes in the price of a market basket of consumer goods and services purchased by households. Changes in the CPI are used as measures of inflation.

How can it impact your investment portfolio?

If the increases in the CPI are small and the expectation of inflation is low, then the equity market and the bond market interpret it in a positive way: low inflation pressures lead to low interest rates. When there are large increases in the CPI, the bond market and the equity market will react negatively: high inflation is expected, which will lead to increased interest rates.

2. The GDP

The gross domestic product (GDP) is a measure of the total market value of all final goods and services produced in a period (quarterly or yearly).

The indicators presented in the Chapter must be analyzed over a period of time, so the direction of their trend is revealed.

How can it impact your investment portfolio?

When GDP growth is healthy and stems from strong business activity, it will lead to higher corporate profits. As a result of the higher profits, the stock market will rise. When the GDP expands less rapidly than the economic predictions, the bond market will rise.

3. Housing starts

Housing starts reflect the number of new, privately-owned houses on which construction has been started in a given period.

How can it impact your investment portfolio?

Changes in the rate of housing starts have a three-dimensional effect: there are more jobs for construction workers — so they have more money to spend; after the home is sold, it generates revenues for the company that built it; and the buyer spends money on furnishing the house - e.g., furniture and appliances.

When housing starts decrease, the bond market rises, because the decrease signals low inflation pressures.

When housing starts increase, the bond market goes down due to the fear of inflation, while stock prices may react in a positive way because corporate profits will rise.

4. Joblessness claims

This report tracks how many new people have filed for unemployment benefits in the previous week.

How can it impact your investment portfolio?

An increasing trend indicates that fewer people have jobs, so their ability to spend money is weakened. On the other hand, a decreasing trend indicates that more people have jobs: every job generates an income that gives the household more spending power, creating a stronger economy with more corporate profits. This is good for the stock market. However, if the number of job seekers is so low that businesses have a hard time finding new workers, then they are forced to spend more on labor costs. This leads to wage inflation, which can be followed by an increase in interest rates, bringing the stock and bond markets down together.

Conclusions concerning your wealth building

Based on economic indicators, investors will try to figure out if the central bank will raise, lower, or not change the interest rate.

As long as investors assume that inflation and interest rates are under control, they will have a tendency to invest in risky assets.

Epilogue

REMEMBER:

You won't get any prizes just
for knowing things.
You'll only be rewarded for your actions
You gained valuable information -
Use it!

If this book has helped you to better understand the process of wealth building, I would highly appreciate your review on Amazon.

Thank you in advance.
Jacob Nayman

A Brief Summary
of
the Book

Wealth Building
Using the Rule of Thirds

Chapter 1:

Wealth Building

Generating long-term income from multiple sources

Invest your money in a way that will create
an income-generating asset.

Chapter 2:

Investor Mindset

Practice safety

Don't make hasty investment decisions.

Practice safety by diversifying your portfolio.

Use the rule of thirds.

Chapter 3:
The Trading Platform
Banks vs. stockbrokers

Low commissions for buying and selling securities
and financial products are very important for
your financial activity.

If the commissions at the bank are too high, consider
working with a big brokerage firm instead.

The advantages of consulting with an adviser lie
mainly in their access to central, sophisticated
sources of important information.

Chapter 4:

Stocks & Bonds

The building blocks of wealth creation

A stock (also known as equity) is a security that represents the ownership of a fraction of a corporation.

A bond is a fixed-income instrument that represents a loan made by an investor to a borrower.

Unlike bonds, company shares have no "guaranteed return."

Chapter 5:

Play It Safe — Diversify

Get higher rewards with minimal risk

**There are two powerful tools to reduce
your portfolio risks:**
The first tool is asset allocation. The second
tool is buying indexes instead of individual stocks.

Greater risks should only be taken if the potential
return is high. If not, the risk should be avoided.

If you invest in individual stocks, you expose yourself to
high risk **without** the reward of higher returns.

Chapter 6:
Buy Index ETFs
Don't pick specific stocks

Buying ETFs on indexes enables you easily to implement the golden rule - "don't put all your eggs in one basket."

Buying ETFs on sectors or indexes diversifies your investments and considerably reduces the volatility of your portfolio.

Buying ETFs on indexes or sectors reduces your fees.

Chapter 7:

Stocks and the Economy

Cyclical and non-cyclical Trends

Cyclical or non-cyclical stocks refers to the correlation between stocks and the economy.

A cyclical trend is the short-term direction of the stock prices in a specific industry.

If we want to take advantage of market volatility, we should concentrate on short-term cyclical sector trends.

Chapter 8:
Define Your Preferences
Amount of money, time frame, and level of risk

The relationship between return and risk is a double-edged sword: to profit more, you have to be willing to take more risk.

The longer the investment horizon, the higher the level of risk you can afford to be exposed to.

When you buy ETFs traded in a foreign country, they will be also influenced by the currency volatility.

Chapter 9:
The Rule of Thirds
Asset allocation

A wise investor will do the following:
Invest one-third in stocks and bonds.
Invest one-third in real estate, commodities
and volatile sectors.
Invest one-third in money and its equivalents.

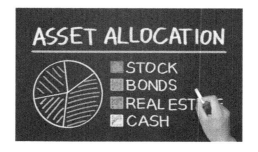

Chapter 10:

Portfolio Construction

Implementing the rule of thirds

Implementing the rule of thirds in your portfolio
will enable you to minimize costs and volatility and
outperform the market benchmark.

Chapter 11:

When is the Right Time to Buy?

"The best chance to deploy capital is when things are going down."

Warren Buffett

If you have the opportunity to buy securities
in a sector or an index at low prices, then increase your
exposure to this index or sector.

Implement Warren Buffet's golden rule:

"Be fearful when others are greedy.
Be greedy when others are fearful."

Chapter 12:

Rebalancing

Preserving the Rule of Thirds

Rebalancing involves periodically buying or selling assets in a portfolio to maintain its original or desired level of asset allocation.

In the process of rebalancing every three months, maintain the rule of thirds.

Chapter 13:

Risk Management

An instrument that protects your money

The general premise of insurance is that you,
as a customer buy peace of mind — while the insurance
company buys your risk.

The protection afforded by insurance
coverage can be considered a risk management
tool that protects your wealth.

Chapter 14:

The Short-Term Profit Strategy

Exploiting cyclical trends

The short-term profit strategy

Buy an ETF on a sector or an index when
its price drops considerably.
Sell the ETF when its price rises considerably.

Chapter 15:

Focus on Sectors or Indexes

Don't pick specific stocks

If you want to create short-term profits, investing your money in indexes and sectors using ETFs is a better strategy than investing in individual stocks.

Deliver alpha by overweighting winning sectors and underweighting losers.

Use ETFs to benefit from the positive interventions made by policy-makers.

Chapter 16:
The Value of Unknown Information
The big advantage

Paradoxically, our ability to profit as investors is increased when we buy stocks without knowing when they will rise again or what exactly will impact them.

When we buy, we assume that something good will happen in the future. We don't know what or when, and neither do the other investors in the market.

Chapter 17:
What is Moving the Markets?
Policy-makers' big impact

If the economy shows signs of an impending economic slowdown/recession, the Federal Reserve will use the QE policy to lower interest rates and positively impact stocks.

If the economy shows signs of overheating that has the potential to lead to inflation pressures, the Federal Reserve will use the QT policy to raise interest rates and negatively impact stocks.

Chapter 18:
Leading Market Indicators:
The impact on interest rates

Based on economic indicators, investors will try to figure
out if the central bank will raise, lower,
or not change the interest rate.

As long as investors assume that inflation and
interest rates are in control, they will have
a tendency to invest in risky assets.

Glossary

A

Active investor

An investor who uses his knowledge to invest money saved by underspending in a private investment portfolio. The portfolio is built in a manner that enables him to minimize costs and volatility and provides him with an opportunity to outperform the market benchmark.

All or nothing strategy

The basic idea behind the "all or nothing" strategy is that the investment company takes significantly more risk than its competitors. As a result, it can produce significantly higher profits. Investors are usually not aware that to achieve these "attractive" results, the company took significant risks with their money.

Alpha returns

The alpha of an investment is the excess return of that investment relative to the return of a benchmark index.

Asset allocation

Asset allocation is the implementation of an investment strategy in an investment portfolio. The strategy attempts to balance between risk and reward by adjusting the percentage of each asset in the investment portfolio according to the customer's personal preferences, the market conditions and the economic environment. The main assumption in asset allocation is that investment in different assets results in portfolio diversification, which reduces the overall risk in the customer investment portfolio while maintaining the expected return level.

Average life of a bond

The average duration, in annual terms, of the bond. The longer the term, the riskier the bond.

B

Balancing an investment portfolio

B alancing your portfolio means buying and selling securities in a way that will return the portfolio to its desired risk levels. They do not have to be the same risk levels you chose when you first built the portfolio.

Benchmark

A benchmark is a standard against which the performance of a mutual fund or the performance of an investment manager can be measured. When evaluating the performance of any investment, it's important to compare it against an appropriate benchmark. For example, to evaluate the performance of your investment manager or your private investment portfolio you can use the S&P 500, the Dow Jones Industrial Average, or the Russell 2000 Index.

Binary options

A binary option is a financial option in which the payoff is either a defined, fixed monetary amount - or nothing at all. Binary options are used in a theoretical framework as the building block for asset pricing and financial derivatives.

Bonds

A loan you give the government or a company. When you hold bonds, you have a chance of receiving the "guaranteed return" even if the company suffers financial difficulties or bankruptcy; the company shareholders, in contrast, can lose all of their money.

Bond rating

A rating which indicates the probability that the borrower (the government / corporation) will meet their obligations and return the invested money plus the promised interest. Corporate bonds are rated according to their level of risk. The rating is given by professional companies that specialize in this area. The rating provides investors with information regarding the risk of investing in the various bonds. If the rating of a bond is low, it means that the risk - the probability that you could lose all your money - is high.

C

Central bank

A central bank is an institution that manages a country's currency, money supply, and interest rates, and uses monetary policy to achieve the objectives of the government. The responsibilities of the central bank include controlling and managing interest rates, setting the reserve requirement, and during times of financial crisis, helping the banking sector to function properly. In most countries, central banks also monitor and supervise financial institutions (including banks) to reduce the risk of reckless or fraudulent activities.

Company shares

Unlike bonds, shares have no "guaranteed return." In other words, they do not guarantee a predictable cash flow to be paid on a specified future date. When you hold shares, you rely on their market value.

Consumer Price Index

The consumer price index (CPI) measures change in the price of a market basket of consumer goods and services purchased by households. Changes in the CPI are used as measures of inflation.

Core-satellite allocation strategy

Core-satellite allocation strategy defines a "core" strategic element that comprises the most significant portion of the portfolio, and applies a dynamic "satellite" strategy to the smaller part of the portfolio. The "core" portion of the portfolio incorporates passive investments that don't require dynamic handling (i.e. index funds, exchange-traded funds (ETFs), mutual passive funds), while the "satellite" portion of the portfolio is composed of investments that demand a more dynamic approach. In the satellite portion, the portfolio is adjusted to include the assets, sectors, or individual stocks that show the most potential for gains. The expectation is that the satellite portion of the portfolio will outperform the market benchmark.

Cyclical stocks

Cyclical stocks and their companies are affected by the economy. When the economy shows positive signs, the price of cyclical stocks will go up. But an economic downturn will have a negative effect on their stock prices.

D

Diversification

"Don't put all your eggs in one basket" is the golden rule. If this rule is not adhered to, there is a risk that the investments will be lost, with no higher probability of returns. Studies have shown that investing in over 20 securities can eliminate the specific risk of an investment portfolio: the only risk that will remain is the market risk. Diversification enables maximum returns with minimum risk.

Durable goods orders

An economic indicator that reflects the number of new orders placed with domestic manufacturers for the delivery of factory hard goods (in the near term or in the future).

E

Entry premium

The difference between the price you could have paid for the stocks at the start of the rise in the Stock Market and the higher price you pay later is called the cover charge, or "entry premium."

ETF

An ETF (exchange traded fund) is a marketable security that tracks an index, a commodity, bonds, or a basket of assets. Like a mutual fund, an ETF is a pool of investments; however, an ETF will often have lower associated costs. Unlike mutual funds, an ETF trades like a common stock on the stock exchange, and its price changes throughout the day as it is bought and sold.

Exotic financial products

Unregulated financial products that contain a lot of false promises. There are financial products that are difficult to understand, introduced as "sexy" and profitable, which are indeed composed of elements that are very profitable - but only to the seller. If you give into temptation and buy them, they can hurt the returns in your investment portfolio.

Exposure to foreign currencies

If you buy a financial product traded in a foreign country, in most cases it will be influenced by the currency exchange of that country. Therefore, buying ETFs on overseas stock indexes, for example, exposes you to foreign currency fluctuations.

F

Federal Reserve

The central banking system of the United States of America.

Fees for securities

The level of commission for buying and selling securities and financial products is very important for your financial activity.

Financial freedom

The ability to produce a steady income and maintain your desired lifestyle even when you don't work.

Financial adviser

The adviser has access to reports prepared by the economics department of the financial institution at which they are employed. These reports can provide essential information on the basis of which, among other things, it can be determined how much foreign currency you should keep in your investment portfolio, and on the basis of which an institutional recommendation can be made regarding the percent to invest in various investment channels.

Financial platforms

A bank, an investment company, or a brokerage firm.

Financial simulators

Used to simulate asset allocations based on customer preferences while taking the macroeconomic conditions in the market into account.

FOMO: The fear of missing out

As investors, we can wait for the economy to heal completely, and only then invest our money in the Stock Market. However, it may take years before the economy is 100 precent healthy. And most investors won't wait due to the fear of missing out.

Forex

The Foreign Exchange global market, where currencies are traded. It is decentralized, meaning there is no central marketplace for foreign exchange; instead, currency trading is conducted electronically, "over the counter" (OTC) - all transactions between traders around the world occur via computer networks. The market is open 24 hours a day except on weekends. The foreign exchange market assists international trade and business by providing a platform for currency conversion.

Future market expectations

If the market expects that the central bank will raise interest rates in the near future, the market will not "wait" until it actually happens - it will react as if the increase in interest rates has already been implemented.

G

GDP

The gross domestic product (GDP) is a measure of the total market value of all final goods and services produced in a period (quarterly or yearly).

Government Bonds

Always safer than corporate bonds: the government can always print more money to meet its obligations, while companies depend on their financial strength to meet their obligations.

H

Housing starts

Housing starts reflects the number of new, privately-owned houses on which construction has been started in a given period.

I

Interest rates

When deciding where to invest your money, you have several alternatives. The solid channel offers investments with only a very low risk; therefore, if interest rates are high, it is preferable to put most of your money in solid investments, such as government bonds.

In such circumstances your investments will enjoy high interest rates, and your level of exposure to risky assets will drop. The opposite is also true: the lower the interest rates are, the more worthwhile it is to take risks in order to generate higher returns; the level of exposure to risky assets, such as stocks, will usually be higher. When interest rates are low the demand for risky assets is higher, and the prices, accordingly, are also higher.

Investment company

An investment company is a corporation or a trust that invests the money of investors in financial securities.

Insurance premiums

An insurance premium is the amount of money an individual or business pays for an insurance policy.

Investment horizon importence

The longer the investment horizon, the higher the level of risk you can afford to be exposed to, since your investments will have plenty of time to ride out the market's short-term fluctuations. Accordingly, the potential to gain higher returns will be greater.

Investor preferences

The portfolio should be built in accordance with investor desires and needs; to accomplish this, the following issues should be addressed: the sum of money to be invested in the private portfolio, the period of the investment, and exposure to risk and the required return.

J

Joblessness claims

This report tracks how many new people filed for unemployment benefits in the previous week.

L

Leading market indicators

An active government has several important economic obligations / objectives that it should actively pursue: high employment, price stability, and economic growth.

Liquidity

Liquidity refers to the portion of the portfolio that you can immediately realize to cash without incurring a loss in returns. Although you receive very low returns from the liquid portion, it's an important part of the overall investment portfolio. The liquidity allows you to act quickly if there are opportunities in the financial market. If you need a high level of liquidity, then cash and cash equivalents can meet this requirement.

M

Market benchmarks

The risky part of the investment is compared to the performance of the Stock Market and high-yield bonds, and the solid part is compared to the benchmark of solid bonds.

"Market portfolio"

A theoretical concept. It is defined as a portfolio consisting of investments that include every financial asset available in the world market. The representation of each asset in the "market portfolio" is proportional to its total presence in the world market. Because its components mirror all of the assets in the financial world, the expected return of the market portfolio should be identical to the expected return of the whole market. Since the market portfolio, by definition, is optimally diversified, it is subject only to risks that affect the whole market, and not to the risks relevant to a particular asset in the portfolio. In the process of building an investment portfolio based on the "market portfolio" concept, investors use proxies for the market portfolio such as the S&P 500 in the US, the FTSE 100 in the UK, the DAX in Germany, and more.

Market volatility

Can be expressed by inflation, deflation, fluctuations in interest rates, currencies and the Stock Market.

Mutual funds

A pool of money from many investors used to purchase securities, which include stocks, bonds, money market instruments and similar assets. In essence, mutual funds are joint investments. When you invest your money in them, they allow you to use licensed portfolio managers to manage your investment and thereby benefit from their knowledge and experience.

Market risk of a security

The product of macroeconomic factors, such as a sharp rise in interest rates, inflation, deflation, a crisis in a major market player (Europe, the United States, or China), and more.

Marketability

The ease with which you can buy and sell securities at market price when you choose to do so.

Monetary policy

In the United States, the Federal Reserve is in charge of the monetary policy. The Federal Reserve has four main economic goals: to achieve maximum employment (close to 95 percent); to maintain stable prices (two — three percent inflation per year); to keep interest rates relatively low; and to provide banks with liquidity that enables them to operate in a "healthy" way. To achieve all four goals the Federal Reserve uses a monetary policy, which is implemented through the actions of the central bank. The main "weapon" used by the Federal Reserve is the control, and if needed, adjustment of the interest rate. It does this by financial actions such as buying or selling government bonds and changing the amount of money that banks are required to keep in their reserves. These actions have far-reaching implications for the economy, as they impact the interest rates on savings accounts, corporate bonds, student loans and mortgages.

N

Non-cyclical stocks

Non-cyclical stocks are profitable regardless of economic trends because they produce or distribute **basic** goods and services that consumers always require.

P

Portfolio manager

Portfolio managers make investment decisions for a fund or group of funds under their control. They base their investment decisions on their evaluation of the financial markets. They buy and sell securities as the conditions in the Stock Market changes.

Q

Quantitative easing (QE)

QE is a monetary policy strategy used by central banks, such as the Federal Reserve. Under QE, a central bank purchases securities in an attempt to reduce interest rates, increase the supply of money and drive more lending to consumers and businesses. The goal is to expand economic activity.

Quantitative tightening (QT)

Quantitative tightening is a contractionary monetary policy applied by a central bank to decrease the amount of liquidity within the economy. The effect of QT is increased interest rates that help to slow or keep the domestic currency from inflation.

R

Rebalancing

Rebalancing involves periodically buying or selling assets in a portfolio to maintain its original or desired level of asset allocation.

Regulated financial product

A regulated financial product must meet three basic conditions:

1. It must be sold by a licensed financial entity, preferably a financial institution (a bank, an investment company), that operates in the country you live in;

2. The money to purchase the product must remain in a bank account registered in your name, i.e. there is no demand that you transfer your money to another account; and

3. The product is simple and easy to understand.

Risk vs. return relationship

Higher returns on investments - higher profits - require more risk.

S

Satellite portion of an investment portfolio

The dynamic element - the satellite portion will be built from actively managed investments. These are investments that do not reflect the "market portfolio."

The goal: The expected returns should outperform the returns of the "market portfolio."

Secular trend

A secular trend is a long-term trend that indicates that a particular sector of the economy is changing.

Specific security risk

Derives from specific negative events such as strikes, mismanagement, embezzlement, or risk that decreases the company's profit due to an unexpected event. This type of risk may lead to a sharp drop in the price of the company's shares.

Sharpe ratio

The Sharpe ratio is a tool for the calculation of risk-adjusted return. The Sharpe ratio can help explain whether a portfolio or investment company that has returns in excess of the benchmark is backed by smart investment decisions or is the result of taking too much risk. A higher Sharpe ratio indicates better performance of the investment manager.

Spot market

The place where currencies are bought and sold according to the current price. The current price is a reflection of many variables. The forwards and the futures markets are used by international corporations to protect themselves against future fluctuations in exchange rates.

Solid bonds

All of the bonds in the solid investment part of the portfolio should meet two criteria: first, the bonds should have an average maturity of up to five years or less. Second, the corporate bonds should have high ratings (AA or higher). Bonds that do not meet those criteria are not considered solid investments.

Structured product

Also known as a market-linked investment, a structured product is created through a process of financial engineering. It is a pre-packaged investment strategy based on a combination of underlying factors such as shares, bonds, indexes or commodities with derivatives (like options, forwards, and swaps).

T

Ticker symbol

Each stock traded on the U.S. stock exchange is associated with a ticker symbol. The ticker consists of a number of letters that are usually reminiscent of the name of the company that issued the shares. The ticker is used by investors in any case in which it is necessary to specify the specific stock,

Transparency

The investment company that sells the financial product is required by law to publish a prospectus before beginning its operations. A prospectus is a document that contains important details for investors, such as specifics regarding investment policies.

U

Ultimatum tactic

I've been given an offer by your competitor. If you can't match it or better, I will transfer my money to him."

V

VIX

The CBOE Volatility Index, known by its ticker symbol VIX, is a popular measure of the Stock Market's expectation of volatility implied by S&P 500 index options. It is calculated and published on a real-time basis by the Chicago Board Options Exchange (CBOE), and is commonly referred to as the "fear index" or the "fear gauge."

Y

Yield to maturity

The annual return of the investor, if the bond is held until its maturity.

Z

Zero sum game

An economic concept according to which one investor's gains must be balanced by another investor's losses.

Made in the USA
Monee, IL
03 November 2022